THE YOUNG ENTREPRENEURS' CLUB

FOOD AND DRINK

MIKE HOBBS

Smart Apple Media

Published by Smart Apple Media
P.O. Box 3263
Mankato, Minnesota 56002
www.blackrabbitbooks.com

U.S. publication copyright © 2014 Smart Apple
Media. International copyright reserved in all
countries. No part of this book may be reproduced
in any form without written permission from the
publisher.

Published by arrangement with the
Watts Publishing Group LTD, London.

Library of Congress
Cataloging-in-Publication Data

Hobbs, Mike, 1954-
Food and drink / by Mike Hobbs.
    p. cm. -- (Young entrepreneurs club)
Includes index.
Summary: "Students interested in the food and
drink marketplace learn what it takes to become
young entrepreneurs in the industry. Successful food
and drink moguls are spotlighted, and step-by-step
instructions are given to jump-start the thought
process of starting a business in the food and drink
industry. Questions throughout the book challenge
critical thinking"--Provided by publisher.

ISBN 978-1-59920-923-4 (library binding)
1. Food industry and trade--Juvenile literature.
2. Hospitality industry--Juvenile literature.
3. Entrepreneurship--Juvenile literature.
I. Title.

HD9000.5.H595 2014
647.95068--dc23
2012040213

Series Editor: Paul Rockett
Consultant: David Gray
Design: Simon Burrough
Picture Research: Diana Morris

Printed in the United States of America
at Corporate Graphics, North Mankato, Minnesota

P01589/2-2013

9 8 7 6 5 4 3 2 1

Picture credits: A-Digit/istockphoto: 18; Africa Studio/
Shutterstock: 22t; Andersontrail.com: 23t, 23c; Xavier
Arnan/istockphoto: 34; Martin Barlow/Art Directors &
TRIP/Alamy: 32tr; Barbro Bergfeldt/Shutterstock: 17t;
Adrian Burke/Alamy: 35b; Canadian Press/Rex Features:
39; Bogdan Carstina/Dreamstime: 24b; Paul Cowan/
Dreamstime: 8; Crisp/Shutterstock: 37 bg; Valeria
Dincu/Dreamstime: 5; Olga Dmitreva/Shutterstock:
26c; Firstflavor.com: 29t, 29c, 29b; David Fisher/
Rex Features: 41; Courtesy of Foodhost.co.uk: 9;
Foodspotting.com: 13; Foodzie.com: 19; Freshii.com:
11; Nick Hanna/Alamy: 30; ibusca/istockphoto: 22c;
innocentdrinks.co.uk: 7, 15t, 15c; Jitalia17/istockphoto:
31c; Michael Jung/Shutterstock: 20; kimandscotts.com:
21t, 21b; Kurij.com: 27; Thomas Lehne/Lotuseaters/
Alamy: 32tl; Leontura/istockphoto: 26t; Torsten Lorenz/
Shutterstock: 35t; Madlen/Shutterstock: 12c; Dean
Mitchell/istockphoto: 28; Anna Nizami/Shutterstock: front
cover c; nomnomtruck.com: 33t, 33c, 33b; Peter Olive/
Photofusion/Alamy: 14; Caitlin Petolea/Shutterstock:37c;
Vikram Raghuvanshi/istockphoto: 40t; Tom Schmucker/
istockphoto: 40b; Shepherdspurse.co.uk: 35c; Dmitry
Shironosov/Shutterstock: 16t; Stocklife/Shutterstock:
24c; StockstudioX/istockphoto: 10c; Michael Stevelmans/
Shutterstock: 38; Dmytro Sukharevskyy/Shutterstock:
10t; Superjam.co.uk: 25 bg, 25t, 25c, 25b; Konstantin
Sutyargin/Shutterstock: 36; Vlue/Shutterstock: 12b;
Valentyn Volkov/Shutterstock: 37t; Volosina/Shutterstock:
17b; Denis Vrublevski/Shutterstock: 17c; Matka Wariatka/
Shutterstock: front cover bg; Feng Yu/Shutterstock: 37b;
Peter Zelei/istockphoto: 31t; Zurijeta/Shutterstock: 16b.

CONTENTS

The Food and Drink Business

We're all involved in the food and drink industry, because everyone needs to eat and drink. Every one of us is a **consumer**, but what's it like to be on the other side?

Food and Drink People

Many people make their living by providing us with food and drink. There are the people involved in farming and growing the many ingredients. Then there are those who make or **process** food and drinks to sell to us in stores. And let's not forget those who work in restaurants, cafés, and bars where we can go and buy meals and drinks.

Facts:

The total worldwide sales of food each year are worth well over $3 trillion.

About one-third ($1 trillion) of that is spent in the US, by far the largest market. $27 billion of this sum is spent on organic products.

On average, Americans consume the most carbonated soft drinks. Here are the top 3 countries for annual soda pop consumption per person:

United States, 45 gallons (170 L)

Mexico, 38.5 gallons (146 L)

Chile, 33.5 gallons (127 L)

In the US, about $115 billion is spent on non-alcoholic drinks.

The food and drink industry may seem crowded: 16.5 million people in the United States work in the food industry alone. This means anyone who wants to enter the industry is getting good news and bad news at the same time. There'll always be a market, but it can be tough to break into.

Even so, you should be positive. People's tastes change year by year. So there's always room for new **products** and **ventures**. A hard-working **entrepreneur** can always find an opportunity .

CHALLENGE

Write a list of all of the things you like most about the food and drink industry. Put the items into an order starting with the item that most interests you. Is there anything you could add to this market area?

Young Entrepreneur
Foodhost

While preparing food in places such as KFC, McDonald's, and Nando's, British student Christopher Tau (left)would spend his time dreaming of dinner parties. Inspired by product sharing sites he'd seen on the Internet, he thought "Why hasn't anybody done this for fine dining?"

At the age of 23, and with the money he'd saved from working in fast food joints, he launched Foodhost. This is a site where people can register to hold or attend dinner parties. Christopher has created a social network for people who love food. Similar businesses already exist within the United States, but this is the first within the UK. There is a risk that it may not succeed, but as Christopher says:

"I believe you should test yourself as much as possible while you're young and I've already learned more lessons during the four months I've spent getting the site off the ground than I did during three years at college."

YOUR THOUGHTS

Why might it be a good idea to launch something new, like Foodhost, rather than repeat a business, like a café, which already exists?

Becoming an Entrepreneur

What is an Entrepreneur?

An entrepreneur is a person who puts time, money, and energy into making a business idea happen and takes a risk that it will be profitable. You can get ideas from anywhere. Which part of the food and drink market are you interested in? Soft drinks? Vegetarian foods? Sandwich bars? Coffee shops? Do you want to provide a product or a service? The list is endless.

What makes a successful entrepreneur?

You may already be familiar with some food and drink entrepreneurs. Some will have their names attached to their products or services. How did they get there and how do you join them? It's down to a mixture of hard work, good taste, and knowing what the public wants. There are certain actions that you must take:

A restaurant can offer many opportunities for business. You may supply a certain type of food, become a chef, or have great ideas for publicity.

- Get some money behind you
- Perfect your product
- Choose a good team
- Develop a **marketing plan**
- Get your venture known
- Don't give up—be persistent!

This book will explore all these points and more in greater detail.

CHALLENGE

Make a list of all the things you think would make a successful entrepreneur. Now make a list of three friends. Which friends have the skills you have listed? Who do you think would be the best entrepreneur?

Young Entrepreneur

Freshii

Sometimes successful risk-taking can be kick-started by bad experiences. Canadian Matthew Corrin (below), who founded Freshii in 2005, was inspired by New York's famous Midtown delis—because he didn't like them. He moved back to Toronto, and convinced his parents he had spotted a gap in the market. With their start-up money to cover rent, equipment, raw materials, and wages, he opened the first Freshii.

He started selling simple, affordable, healthy meals, consisting of soup, a wrap, and salads. Matthew wanted to do away with the excuse that people don't eat well because there's nothing convenient or affordable. He claims the day he opened Freshii was the first day he ever worked in the restaurant or retail business.

He admits that, in an ideal world, he would probably have done things differently, but there is no doubt he showed the right risk-taking spirit.

The risk that he took has had its reward. Now he has head offices in Chicago and 50 Freshii stores, with plans to open 650 more.

YOUR THOUGHTS

Why do you think Matthew was successful? What could he have done differently?

The Vital Spark

Finding Ideas

Where can you get your ideas from? For food and drink, many ideas come directly from personal experience. Let's say you really enjoy some foods but have an allergy to certain ingredients these foods contain. That might well inspire you on to come up with a new product.

Or perhaps you've been working in a shop or restaurant and you see something missing you believe the public would really enjoy. Many young entrepreneurs have gotten started by spotting a gap in the market in this way.

You might even have a brainstorm as a result of your hobbies or passions. For instance, you're a fisher and come up with some new snack that will stay fresh longer near water. Maybe an idea just comes to you right out of the blue, whether you're searching for one or not.

The crucial thing is you believe in it and pursue it with passion.

Give yourself half an hour to think about new food or drink products you could develop and write them down. Choose the one that most interests you for your business idea.

CHALLENGE

Ideas often come from filling a need that we have ourselves —be it a particular service we want or flavor of ice cream we love!

Young Entrepreneurs

Foodspotting

Foodspotting was founded by Alexa Andrzejewksi and Ted Grubb (with Soraya Darabi who joined later) in San Francisco in 2009. It is an iPhone application and website that allows users to post and discover nearby restaurant dish recommendations through photographs. The spark that got it going was eating new food in different countries. When that was linked to the swiftly growing app market, the interest in photographing food, and the huge rise in social networks, they had a success on their hands.

Alexa first came up with the idea for Foodspotting when she traveled to Japan and Korea and discovered lots of foods she'd never heard of before. She returned to San Francisco and was unable to find them there. She set out to create a better way for people to learn about new foods and to find them locally. Ted convinced her that a photo-sharing location app was the best way forward. Ted developed the app himself and they brought in Soraya's social networking skills (all the way from New York) to make it happen. They now have offices in both cities.

YOUR THOUGHTS

There are four things that contributed to the vital spark for Foodspotting. What are they? Which do you think was most important?

Market Research

Researching Your Market

Well, you love your idea, obviously. Now it's time to research what people think about your plan. You need to ask yourself: will you be able to find people to buy what you're selling? If you want to open a sandwich counter, are you choosing a location where there are plenty of hungry office workers? If it's a restaurant, are you sure that people within your area can afford to eat out?

You've got to do some **market research** and there are two main types: **Primary research** involves walking around and finding out new information for yourself. **Secondary research** involves discovering facts that already exist, from a library or the Internet.

◀ **Stopping people in the street to ask them questions is a form of primary research.**

The Right Questions

You must establish that there is really a need for your product or service by asking the right questions. What do customers want? How many of them can you hope to attract? Do they like your idea? Perhaps get some of your friends to help you with asking the questions in a shopping street or mall. It might help if you have an example of your product for people to try.

How do you find out if your business idea is a good one? Think of some ways you can test your market without spending a lot of money.

CHALLENGE

your daily fruit

CAUTION
fresh fruit
in transit

innocent

Young Entrepreneurs
Innocent Drinks

We all love drinking healthy, delicious fruit smoothies, and Innocent Drinks has been one of the biggest success stories in the UK market. From a small start in 1999, the company now sells two million drinks a week.

Richard Reed, Adam Balon, and Jon Wright (above), who created Innocent Smoothies, had a great way of testing how good they were and whether there was a market for them.

At a music festival where they were selling their drinks, they asked customers to answer the question "Should we give up our day jobs?" by putting empties in YES or NO baskets.

The response they received was clear. When they checked at the end of the festival, the YES basket was full and the NO basket had only three empties. They all resigned and the next day started working on Innocent Smoothies seriously. They were soon helped by an American businessman investing $400,000.

YOUR THOUGHTS

Were they wise to just test their drinks at a music festival? Where else could they have done this?

Bringing in the Money

Getting Started

Once you've finished your research, you'll need to find some money to cover **costs**. You can get a loan at a bank, ask friends, relatives, and business contacts (backers). They'll probably want some of your **profits** in return, but it's worth it!

Whoever gives you funds, they'll need a clear idea of how you are going to make money. Figure out all your **costs** and show how much you hope to sell. This will give them an idea of when they might get their money back!

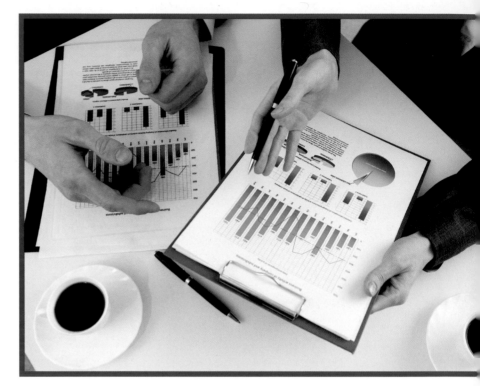

▲ **Graphs and pie charts are a good way to display your budget.**

Making a Profit

As soon as you've found the money to develop your plans, calculate the amount of money you expect to spend and receive (your **budget**). Include all the costs you'll have to pay and be realistic about your sales. Your profit is the money you bring in less your costs. It won't matter how good your product is if you can't make money on it.

CHALLENGE

Where can you get money from to develop your idea? Draw up a list of everyone you might ask—and don't forget the obvious people!

Young Entrepreneur

Lime Fresh Mexican Grill

John Kunkel was 29 when he opened his first Lime Fresh Mexican Grill in 2002 in South Beach, Miami, a year after starting his bakery Taste, and after ten years working for others in the restaurant business. The start-up funding he needed was considerable, and he had to raise money by borrowing against his home, pushing his credit cards to the limit, and borrowing from his friends to cover all his costs.

He estimated the total start-up costs at $524,000. Many people never get to open their dream restaurants because they underestimate these costs. Construction and improvements were about $430,000; one month's rent, deposit, and utilities about $25,000; insurance, permits, and technology about $32,000; and marketing and advertising roughly $37,000. However, the surge in social networking has meant these marketing and **advertising** costs can now be scaled down.

Thankfully, the gamble worked. John now has ten Lime restaurants throughout Florida, and is looking to add **franchises** elsewhere.

YOUR THOUGHTS

If you had to raise the start-up funds that John needed, would you go about it in the same way?

Product Development On the Go

Perfect Your Design

It's pretty rare to get every single piece of your plan right the first time. Be prepared to experiment. You need to design your product or your store (or get someone else to do it for you) so it tastes and looks as perfect as it possibly can.

Preparing Food or Drink

Your research will have given you some good ideas about what customers are looking for. Use these to improve your product so that it suits consumers' tastes and not just your own. Make sure that the packaging is both attractive and right for your product.

Opening a Store or Café

Again, you will now have a better idea of what your customers might want. Lay out your store so that it invites people in and is easy to move around once they're inside. Try things out and see what you can improve still further. Now's the time to develop your idea. Everything must be ready to go when you decide to launch.

CHALLENGE

Think about a food and drink product you know. What's good about the **packaging, taste, look,** etc? What can be done to make it even better? Write down as many different improvements as you can think of.

Young Entrepreneurs

Foodzie

Foodzie was launched in San Francisco in 2008 by former Virginia Tech classmates Nik Bauman, Emily Olson, and Rob LaFave (below). Foodzie is an online marketplace for **sustainable** food products, designed to give small food producers a way to sell their goods beyond their local communities. The idea originally came from Emily working as a manager for a large food chain. She saw just how hard it was for small food producers to sell their goods to big retailers.

But Foodzie wouldn't have been successful if they hadn't provided a good service. The key to this was that they increased the number of products they sold to attract customers and keep them coming back. The company offers many food products that consumers cannot find anywhere else. Tasters test all the products and only put them on sale if they are enthusiastic about them. People know they can rely on Foodzie to market a range of high-quality foods, many of them unique.

YOUR THOUGHTS

Do you think Foodzie's product development and range extension is a good idea? Why?

Hygiene and Service Issues

Preparation Standards

The risk of getting sick from eating or drinking is always there. So when you're preparing food or drink to be packaged and sold, you must be very alert about **hygiene** from the start. Think about your product. Is it safe and is it made and displayed in a hygienic way?

Service Standards

If you want to sell food or drink in any form to the public for consuming on the spot, you must also follow strict hygiene standards. If your idea for a business is a store, a restaurant, or café, is it clean and customer-friendly? What about the hygiene aspects of preparation, storage, and display? Take plenty of time to get these things right. It's very important you do so.

Organizations such as the Food and Drug Administration set these standards and make sure that all companies stick to them. The inspections and regulations might seem excessive, but they are set to ensure your product is safe for all your customers.

CHALLENGE

You are opening a sandwich shop. What are the main safety issues that there might be in preparing the food and serving it to customers?

If you are working in a kitchen it is important that cleaning standards are high.

Young Entrepreneurs
Kim & Scott's Gourmet Pretzels

Kim and Scott Holstein founded Kim & Scott's Gourmet Pretzels in 1995 when they couldn't find any of the types of pretzels they wanted to eat in their home city of Chicago. In true entrepreneurial fashion they decided to make and market some themselves. Starting out with no pretzel knowledge —they were running an ice cream franchise at the time—they soon discovered proper preparation was vital to success. They have gone from strength to strength (annual sales are between $10 million and $15 million) and recently decided to introduce a gluten-free pretzel to their product line.

There were obviously many hygiene-related issues involved if they were to market their new product with confidence. However, Kim & Scott's had great experience in this field: they have been baking nut-free pretzels for 15 years. In order to do this, they have been preparing these pretzels in a totally nut-free kitchen facility throughout that time. It's been a simple matter to extend the use of this kitchen, and now each gluten-free soft pretzel is also made by hand in this hygienic environment.

YOUR THOUGHTS

What could happen if Kim & Scott's did not follow good standards of hygiene?

Packaging and Shelf Life

Packaging

Well, it may be hygienic and look great, but can your business survive the rough and tumble of everyday use? If it's a product that could suffer damage, will the packaging protect it properly? The purpose of packaging is to make sure that your product can be sold in perfect condition. Types of packaging range from egg cartons to cans, from bottles to boxes.

Shelf Life

The other thing that the packaging must do is to give important information to anyone buying your product. On every food or drink item on sale you may see a "use by" or "best before" date so consumers know by when the product should be eaten. This also explains the importance of **shelf life** for retailers, who sell their products before these dates.

What else do you have to cover to make sure your product can be sold?

◄ **"Best before" information is usually printed on the back or bottom of products.**

Make certain you list all the ingredients and, as a bonus, make sure they boost your sales prospects. Healthy ingredients can be a strong way of advertising your product. And of course don't forget, your packaging must be attractive!

CHALLENGE

Imagine you're launching a new health food. Put down all the ingredients and write two sentences saying why it will help people stay healthy.

Young Entrepreneur

Anderson Trail

Justin Anderson (right) found that many granola products on the market were neither tasty nor healthy. So he started making his special granola for his family and friends when he was just 16 after finding one he loved on a New Mexico camping trip. Everyone seemed to like it and things just grew from there. After researching the competition in local health food shops, Justin knew he had a good chance of doing well.

Eight years later, he is running Anderson Trail and selling his Original Premium Moist with continuing success. Justin's recipe makes granola to the same standard as he found on that early camping trip. The key is having the best ingredients that are low-fat, contain no **cholesterol**, give people a good source of fiber, and yet taste delicious.

As well as offering a product that's tasty, Justin is able to **promote** the health benefits of his granola in his packaging design. He has also introduced a new **venture** where he can **customize** small bags for companies to use as gifts. They can introduce their own logo and message to fit with the Anderson Trail design.

YOUR THOUGHTS

Look at the Anderson Trail packaging and write a list of why the packaging works and looks good to customers.

Know Your Competition

Gathering Information

It's time to get out and about and find out what else is happening. Who are you up against? The problem in business is that it's not just about your own ideas. Others are often doing something similar and this is especially true in the food and drink industry. Some companies will have customer loyalty from the very customers that you want.

Strengths and Weaknesses

Check out your **rivals** to see what they are doing well. Go in to their restaurant or café and have a meal. Visit their counter and have a drink. Buy their products and try them out. Find out their strengths.

Equally, spot where their weaknesses are. Then you can show people you're offering a better product or service. If they're selling online, order from them. How quick and satisfactory is the service? Can you do better?

◀ **Are your competitors online? Check out what kind of service they're providing.**

▼ **Sometimes your rival may be working just across the street from you.**

CHALLENGE

Think about what you'd like to do, and list all the competitors you'll have. Say why your product is better.

Young Entrepreneur

SuperJam

Growing up in Edinburgh, Scotland, Fraser Doherty (bottom right) always loved the jams that his grandmother used to make. Trying out other jams, that were on the market, he was convinced that her recipes had far more flavor. When he was 14 he got his granny to teach him how she did it.

He learned fast, quickly began to sell the jams, and soon started gaining great publicity. Thinking he might get serious, he took a loan of $8,000 from the Prince's Trust (a charity that invests in youth projects) and convinced a factory and advertising agency to come on board. They gave him their services free at this stage because they could sense profits in the future.

Researching the market in more depth before he went ahead, he discovered jam had an old-fashioned, unhealthy image because it was made with so much sugar. Fraser's SuperJam products, in contrast, are made from fruit juice with no added sugar. As a result of this mixture of tasty and healthy eating, SuperJam is expanding each year, unlike its competitors.

SuperJam™
raspberry and cranberry
100% pure fruit spread

SuperJam™
blueberry and blackcurrant
100% pure fruit spread

YOUR THOUGHTS

Think about other products similar to SuperJam. What does SuperJam have going for it that its competition doesn't?

Building a Team

Selection and Communication

Business is about working with people. You can't always do it alone. That means you have to get a good team together to work with you.

The people you work with must be enthusiastic, reliable, and able to do what you need. Are any of your friends or family interested? You're going to be with these people a great deal so it helps if you already get along. Of course, they also have to be the best people for the job.

It's important for all members of a team to listen to each other.

Think about the roles that need filling and what part of the business you want to be involved in. If you're opening a restaurant how important is it for you to be the head chef? You may have to interview people to fill certain jobs in your team. List what their responsibilities will be, and what type of person you want.

If you've chosen well, the team may be able to provide some new ideas that help your business.

CHALLENGE

Many companies have team building exercises to get people working well together. Think about a game to play with your team and why this would be beneficial.

Young Entrepreneurs

Kurij

Kurij (pronounce it like "courage") is the result of the coming together of Alex Deo, Dr. Tung Bui, and Alex Tai (left) in Phoenix, Arizona. Alex Deo, a student dentist, met Dr. Bui to shadow him for a day. They discovered a shared interest in dreaming up new products. Alex's idea for tube socks soon lost out to his plans for a revolutionary soft drink.

They decided they wanted to make a new soft drink that had to do three things. It had to be healthy and tooth friendly, so it had to have natural ingredients. It had to quench your thirst properly. And it had to taste really good. They worked on this until their drink was perfected. Then they met the third team member, Alex Tai, who loves start-ups.

So the two-strong team became three. Kurij was launched onto the market in 2009. Because it met the three goals its creators had set and their skills support each other, it has proved to be very successful.

YOUR THOUGHTS

What did each of these team members bring to the company?

Leading from the Front

Becoming a Leader

You can go to lots of places to find good tips on picking up leadership skills. Find out about those who have made it big in the food and drink industry, then look for information on other leaders, such as business leaders, sports coaches, and politicians.

You will find that everyone who works with you will be different. You will need to inspire your team in the ways that suit them. You may need to be flexible and you must certainly listen to what they say. But when it comes down to making the final decision, it is likely to be yours and yours alone.

Managing Time

Leaders need time to make decisions, and one of your hardest tasks will be to manage your time. One suggestion is to make it a **priority** that you have, say, an hour each working day when you are free to think without interruptions.

Are you a confident speaker who can present in front of a group? As a leader, you may have to be.

CHALLENGE

You are due to launch your product and your sales team need to be briefed today. However, your finance director wants you to visit the bank for a meeting. What do you decide, and why?

Young Entrepreneurs

First Flavor

Adnan Aziz had just graduated from the University of Pennsylvania when he was watching *Charlie and the Chocolate Factory* and loved the scene where people licked the walls and tasted fruit. He decided to try to invent something just like that, and came up with small soluble flavor strips that did the trick.

He was aware that this was a huge invention for the food and drink industry and it would need experienced leadership to grow to its **potential**. So he met up with Josh Kopelman, a successful entrepreneur (he had been Entrepreneur of the Year for Greater Philadelphia) to form First Flavor. Supported by Jay Minkoff, they patented the Peel 'n Taste Marketing System. Now new tastes in food and drink can be tried out in all types of print media and promotions. Josh and Jay had helped provide the leadership that would help First Flavor succeed.

YOUR THOUGHTS

Why do you think Adnan needed the leadership of others to advance his product?

Make a Marketing plan

Using the Four Ps

It's hard to succeed without a clear marketing plan. This is important within the food and drink industry, where you will face a lot of competition for attention. Draw up a plan that spells out how you're going to get the best possible sales. It should include all the things you will do in every part of the marketing mix (often called the four Ps).

- **Product:** What is it that makes your product original? This may be expressed in a phrase that can be used as an advertising **slogan**. Is the food used seasonally—can this be an advantage?
- **Price:** Remember, the price at which you choose to sell your product is crucial. Make it too high and you risk losing sales. Make it too low and you lose profits (and make what you're offering seem less valuable).
- **Place:** Where people can buy what you're selling. Where is the best place to sell popcorn?
- **Promotion:** All the ways you can use to get people to notice and try your product. Is it worth organizing a free tasting session?

Once you have written your plan, use it as a guide to follow. Make sure the plan is closely linked to your budget. Don't commit yourself to advertising you can't afford.

CHALLENGE

Choose a food product or service that you are going to sell. Which of the four Ps do you think is likely to be most important, and why?

Company Focus

The Supermarket Price Wars

The UK supermarket company Tesco originally made its name as a low-cost seller of grocery goods, but as the company grew, it changed. The focus became less on price and more on quality.

However, within the last five years, competition within the UK market has increased. The arrival of budget stores means companies are now offering products much more cheaply than Tesco. The takeover of Asda by the US giant Wal-Mart raised the competition stakes and other leading supermarkets soon started cutting their prices.

This attack on price happened at the same time as the world economy was deep in trouble. Even though Tesco had the most stores, it began to lose its share of the market. So the company responded by starting a major **price war** with the goal of keeping its leading position. The moral? However big you are, you must always look at every part of the marketing mix. It is notable however, that Wal-Mart has not taken part in US supermarket price wars that also began late in 2011.

YOUR THOUGHTS

What do you think would have happened to Tesco had they not cut the cost of their products?

Getting Known

Advertising, PR, and Promotion

Does everyone know about your product? Make sure your advertising is in the right place and reaching the right people. You might want to use TV, radio, newspapers, or magazines. But choose carefully; they can be expensive.

Where is the best place for you to advertise? On the side of a van? A billboard?

Happily, there are other ways to promote your product. Today you can advertise on the Internet or create your own website fairly cheaply. You can also let people know what you are planning to do by sending out a **press release**. If you have an interesting story to tell about a new product you should gain good **media coverage**. Creating a good reputation for your product is known as **public relations (PR)**.

Social media networks, such as Facebook and Twitter, can be important for getting people to find out about your venture. You can easily shoot a short video, put it on YouTube, and quickly gain plenty of hits.

How should the ad look? If it's a drink, you'll want people to look at it and feel thirsty. Having it photographed with water droplets on the bottle in the sun may make people want to reach out and drink it.

CHALLENGE

You are about to launch a new take-out food business and you need to make people aware of it. How would you promote this venture?

YOUR THOUGHTS

How might Nom Nom Truck choose to use their TV appearance within their advertising?

Young Entrepreneurs
Nom Nom Truck

Jennifer Green and Misa Chien (right) noticed that there was a lack of Vietnamese food in Los Angeles, California, so they decided to fix that. They used $25,000 of personal savings and family investments to buy a truck, equipment, and food ingredients. Calling it the Nom Nom Truck, they began selling tasty *banh mi* (special Vietnamese sandwiches) at different LA locations, and customers ate them up.

At first, their main way of reaching their customers was through Twitter and Facebook. They would announce where they were going to be and soon got a loyal following (now 22,000 on Twitter and 13,000 on Facebook). Their main problem was that they were always likely to pick up parking tickets.

But it was their inclusion in a reality TV program, *The Great Food Truck Race*, that gained them tons of new fans. Now, having bought another vehicle, they have increased their takings to $1.2 million in 2011, and are looking at expanding further.

The Launch Day

Off with a Bang!

You're ready at last. Launch your product, and make as big a splash as you can. Try to organize a special event if your budget allows (and it should). It doesn't have to be costly, but it must be fresh, relevant, and exciting. There are many food and drink-related trade fairs which can be ideal places for a launch.

Social media networks must be buzzing with the date you've set. In the same way, any advertising you do must be focused around the launch day. And, of course, all the traditional forms of PR must do the same thing. You're looking for maximum **exposure**.

Any other promotions should either concentrate on the day or run from the day of the launch for a short time. This is when you have a great chance to get people to try your product.

Review what you've done as soon as you can. Are things going according to plan? If there are any **hitches**, be sure to take care of them as quickly as possible, because first impressions really do count. A great launch can really help an outlet or product, but it takes a while to overcome problems on the day itself.

CHALLENGE

You are going to throw a party to launch a line of Halloween cakes. List all the things you could do to make it memorable and exciting.

Inspiring Entrepreneur

Shepherds Purse

Judy Bell (right), married to farmer Nigel in Yorkshire, England, was working part-time in an osteopathy clinic to boost their income. She noticed that many people had a bad reaction to dairy products, especially cheese. Spotting a gap in the market, she produced her first cheese at home from ewes' milk (Yorkshire Fettle) in 1987. Strong sales encouraged her, and she launched her company—Shepherds Purse—and her next cheese —Olde York—in 1989 at the Great Yorkshire Show.

Launching a product at a food or drink trade show is an excellent way of attracting a healthy proportion of your target market. It gives you instant publicity and also makes sure that many of the tastemakers and opinion formers in your industry are there to take notice. It certainly worked for Judy, because her cheeses were an immediate success. That same year, she won the Gold Award at the Nantwich International Cheese Fair, and her company has never looked back.

YOUR THOUGHTS

Why was it a good idea for Judy to launch her company at the Great Yorkshire Show?

Running the Business

Keeping a Close Eye on Sales

Once you've launched, things don't stop there. You will now be planning for future sales as well as running a daily business. From the very first day, check all the **sales figures** regularly and carefully. You have to see that all the money coming into the business is enough to cover the money going out.

Wholesale/Retail

These are the two different parts of the business. Wholesale is where you do not sell your goods to the people who are going to consume your products. Instead you sell to shops, supermarkets, restaurants. Retailing means that you are selling your food and drinks from a fixed point. It could be a shop, a café, a counter, or an online site.

Distribution Channels

These are the ways in which you choose to put your goods into customers' shopping baskets, either by wholesale or retail. Are the distribution channels that you've chosen doing the right job for you? Are you in the right stores? Maybe you could do better in others. Are your likely customers buying? See what you can do to reach them if they're not. Never be afraid to change things if they're not going smoothly.

Supply

The supply chain is the process you set up to make sure you get everything your business needs, from the supply of materials to customer delivery. If you're running a restaurant, is the supply chain that you've set up working properly? You may be able to get ingredients more cheaply from other **suppliers**. Think what you can do to change things if they're not working.

Goods are often transported by large trucks, trains and, if going overseas, cargo ships.

CHALLENGE

You're not making quite the number of sales you expected. What should you do? Should you adjust your targets? Or is that just being negative?

Young Entrepreneurs

Fenugreen

Kavita Shukla and Swaroop Samant founded Fenugreen in Cambridge, Massachusetts in 2010. Fenugreen FreshPaper is a revolutionary form of packaging that keeps fruits and vegetables fresher for longer. Fenugreen extends shelf life naturally by slowing the bacterial and fungal growth that spoils food. It is 75% as effective as refrigeration but not as expensive.

As well as selling online through their own website, Fenugreen has extended their sales outlets by building up a list of distributors to sell FreshPaper for them. They aim to bring in one brand new distributor each week. Because the product is environmentally friendly, it's largely marketed to retailers and growers of organic produce who need to package their goods without using chemicals. It's proved to be very popular with farming organizations, and a large portion is sold through co-op markets.

YOUR THOUGHTS

Why is it good for Fenugreen to be selling their product through outlets other than their website?

Turning Problems into Gains

Problem Solving

So you've launched, sales are great, money's coming in and all's right with the business. Of course, unless you are very lucky, this will probably be the time when certain things start to go wrong.

A vital person gets sick, there's a power outage affecting your online sales, a van breaks down, or there's a strike in your neighborhood. Some things are beyond your control and you have to try to get around them as best you can.

However, there will be some problems that you can control. Your bottled drink reacts badly to heat, customers complain about your slow service, the packaging you use is affecting the taste of your products. These are things you can sort out.

Don't be put off by **setbacks**. Nearly everyone has them at the start of their business careers. The vital thing is to learn from your mistakes. Just make a few adjustments to your product, your plan, or your type of operation and try again. The key is never to give up!

You're stuck in traffic and will be late for a meeting. What should you do?

CHALLENGE

You've been told to withdraw your product for safety reasons. How can you turn this to your advantage? Should you offer a replacement or think about relaunching your product?

Inspiring Entrepreneur
Gordon Ramsay

Gordon Ramsay (right) is one of the most well-known British chefs and food entrepreneurs in the world today. He is famous not just for the quality of his cooking, but also for his many well-publicized TV appearances. However, it has not been a story of continued success. In fact, his career has been controversial and there have been restaurant closures, lawsuits, and family issues that have caused him problems.

But he always bounces back. He is aware that not all restaurants will succeed, and doesn't let it get him down. A continual program of new restaurants opening means that he is always trying out new ideas and adding some finishing touches to old ones. As well as restaurants in the US and the UK, he now has places in Australia, Canada, South Africa, Qatar, Dubai, Japan, and France.

Even the most well-known entrepreneurs suffer troubles from time to time. It's how you react to them that matters.

YOUR THOUGHTS

Do you think problems can be turned into good publicity? How?

Always Look for Ways to Expand

Moving Ahead

Your hard work has been rewarded with success! Your sandwich bar's a smash hit, your organic foods are very popular, your natural energy drinks are front-runners. But don't stand still. Think of ways in which you can build on that success and expand your business. Here are some points on what to do next (with some things to beware of as well).

Let's say you've started by selling only one product. What have customers told you about why they like it, and other things they're looking for? Look at ways you might be able to extend this into a whole line of products that respond to some of their suggestions. Can you do it easily without it costing too much?

Or if you've opened a restaurant or café, is there any potential to open another branch nearby or in a similar town? It should be in a place where you can keep an eye on things: it might be best not to do too much too soon.

Growth

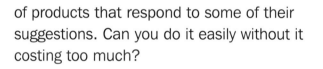

Think about your idea for a moment. When it's successful, what would you most like to do next?

CHALLENGE

Young Entrepreneur

Sam Stern

Sam Stern (left) published his first cookbook at the age of fourteen. He wrote it for kids the same age as himself, who enjoyed eating similar things and were eager to start cooking. Since then he has published four more cookbooks, each reflecting the tastes and situations of his age group as they get older.

Writing for kids his age means that he knows his market well. While he was studying at college, he was able to research material for his fourth book, *Sam Stern's Student Cookbook*. Being a student gave him firsthand experience as to the needs of other students living at college on a budget.

He has supported his book with a website that fits his market audience, offering free recipes, videos, and a blog. These efforts have attracted a loyal fan base. He is constantly researching new recipe ideas and one day hopes to run a restaurant.

YOUR THOUGHTS

How else could Sam develop his business beyond cookbooks and a restaurant?

Glossary

advertising Images and text that interest people in your product or business.

budget The amount of money you expect to spend and receive.

cholesterol A fatty chemical, too much of which can be dangerous.

consumer Anyone who might buy your product.

costs Everything you must spend to make sales.

customize To make something for a particular customer's need.

entrepreneur Someone who takes a financial risk in order to make a profit.

exposure The amount of media coverage your product or business receives.

franchise The right to market and sell someone's product.

hitches Problems or difficulties.

hygiene Standards of cleanliness which people in the industry must follow.

launch The moment you open your business or start selling your product.

marketing plan Describing your likely customers and the things you'll do to sell to them.

market research Finding out if there's a market for your idea, or how it's doing.

media coverage What TV, newspapers, and radio write about your business.

packaging How your product is presented to the consumer.

potential How much you might be able to do or sell.

press release Telling the TV, newspapers, and radio what you plan to do.

price war Cutting prices to take business away from competitors.

priority The thing(s) that you must do first.

profit The amount of money you receive for sales, less the cost of making them.

process How a task is carried out or how something is made.

products The goods or service that you make or produce for consumers to buy.

promote Put your product or business in the minds of likely customers.

public relations (PR) The work you do to give yourself a good reputation.

raw materials Everything you need to make your products.

review Look again at how you're doing things.

rivals Everyone who is competing with you to sell to consumers.

sales Everything you sell to consumers.

sales figures The total amount of sales reported regularly.

setbacks Problems you have in running your business.

shelf life The amount of time you have to sell your product.

slogan Memorable words describing your product.

soluble Able to be dissolved (usually in water).

start-up costs The money you need to find to begin your business.

suppliers People from whom you buy goods or raw materials.

sustainable Something that can be done for a long time.

venture A project that is risky, but could be very worthwhile.

Further Information

Web Sites of Featured Entrepreneurs

Anderson Trail **andersontrail.com/**
Fenugreen **www.fenugreen.com/**
First Flavor **www.firstflavor.com/**
Foodhost **www.foodhost.co.uk/**
Foodspotting **www.foodspotting.com/**
Foodzie **http://foodzie.com/**
Freshii **http://www.freshii.com/**
Gordon Ramsay **www.gordonramsay.com/**
Innocent Drinks **http://innocentdrinks.co.uk/**

Kim and Scott's Gourmet Pretzels
www.kimandscotts.com/
Kurij **www.kurij.com/k/**
Lime Fresh Mexican Grill
www.limefreshmexicangrill.com
Nom Nom Truck **http://nomnomtruck.com/**
Sam Stern **www.samstern.co.uk/**
Shepherds Purse **www.shepherdspurse.co.uk/**
SuperJam **www.superjam.co.uk/**

Other Web Sites

www.fda.gov
The Food and Drug Administration web site provides information on food safety
for those in the food industry and the consumer.

www.youngentrepreneur.com/
Online forum for information and advice on being a young entrepreneur.

Books

Built for Success: The Story of Coca-Cola by Valerie Bodden (Creative Education, 2009)
Built for Success: The Story of McDonald's by Sara Gilbert (Creative Education, 2009)
In the Workplace: Hospitality and Catering Careers by Cath Senker (Amicus, 2011)

Note to Parents and Teachers: every effort has been made by the publishers to
ensure that these web sites are suitable for children, and that they contain no inappropriate
or offensive material. However, because of the nature of the Internet, it is impossible to
guarantee that the contents of these sites will not be altered.

Index